OI YOU LOT

Kareem Parkins-Brown is a writer and visual artist from Grahame Park Estate, NW9. Kareem is a proud Barbican Poet Alumnus. He was almost Young Poet Laureate for London, was shortlisted for the Jerwood Compton Poetry Fellowship and won the Roundhouse Poetry Slam. In 2024 he toured a solo show, *Bougie Lanre's Boulangerie* with Talawa Theatre Company. Kareem's happiest when watching Mean Girls or Carlito's Way.

First published in 2024 by Little Betty, an imprint of Bad Betty Press
Cobden Place, Cobden Chambers, Nottingham NG1 2ED

badbettypress.com

PB ISBN: 978-1-913268-64-0
EPUB ISBN: 978-1-913268-65-7

A CIP record of this book is available from the British Library.

Book design by Amy Acre
Cover artwork by Kareem Parkins-Brown

Supported using public funding by
ARTS COUNCIL
ENGLAND
LOTTERY FUNDED

'Parkins-Brown is the lightkeeper of hood surrealism – strange, lovingly reverent, confident and magnificent – through his work we look towards the slippages of a space that sends you in many directions and see the shapeshifters who make their presences known in and at whatever ends. It feels ours. I didn't want to finish it, I didn't want to give it back. Whatever canon he is part of, we'd be lucky to join him. My heart runs to Kareem's poems, to Kareem's worlds. His poems mean the world to me.' Tice Cin

'There is no writer like Kareem Parkins-Brown. He is vital to the poetry ecosystem because his work is playful and sharp with inventive technicalities – how exciting to see new pathways through the forest of the British canon. *Oi You Lot* is the tender within the storm, it is written at the pulse of the moment where everything is happening at once – grief, humour – his poems stitch seemingly opposing notions together as they hurl you through the tapestry of his London state of living.' Caleb Femi

'Kareem Parkins-Brown's excellent pamphlet is like a funeral held in a bouncy castle: the line-breaks slip on their own tears, jumping mourners get bruised by their collisions and the laughing starts to sound a lot like crying.' Caroline Bird

'I have been waiting for this book for years. There's no voice like Kareem Parkin-Brown's. Sacred and profane, these are critical, kinetic poems for, and of, right now.' Rachel Long

'Kareem Parkins-Brown is one of the most beloved wordsmiths on the London poetry circuit. *Oi You Lot* will show its readers why.' Raymond Antrobus

Oi You Lot

KAREEM
PARKINS-BROWN

LITTLE BETTY

CONTENTS

A gunfinger is just
a middle finger and an index finger.
My anger has a point to it.

LONDON SONNET 2

I am a good Christian boy. I only sin
with other Christians. The wine I drink
gets converted by the Christ in me. The only
swears I say are holyshit! and fuckinghell.
Because I'm sure even Jesus would fuck hell.
I was always a good Christian boy.
When we robbed the pastor's house
we let him put clothes on. He was in a jacuzzi
making bubbles by talking out of his ass. We threw
him off the balcony. His following Sunday
sermon is on How to Survive a Fall
and in my notes the word sermon
keeps changing into demon.
The pastor was once a good Christian boy.

PRESCRIPTION

call God a wasteman then walk between lightning bolts
run through a forest while on fire
lift weights that could crush you
cradle a molotov cocktail like a baby
find the sofa the Simpsons sat on
pick a fight with yourself and win
shout PUSSYOLE at your reflection
bet your fingers at the blackjack table
prick a finger and paint yourself
hike a mountain with somebody you don't like
cradle a baby like a molotov cocktail
buy a house for yourself and your ting
argue with your neighbour
find a black flight attendant to take you to the pilot
challenge him to rock paper scissors as you fly over
    a country at war

GOOD PARENTING

What do you have for lunch today, Peter?
    He holds up a photo of his child and a Bible.
Ah, a picture of Kenny and a picture of God.

        In fact three photos of Kenny. I'm trying to be
        three times the father I currently am. And a Bible,
        I'm trying to be his holy father.

    Before he gets into the story of the prodigal son
I ask what his paternal philosophy is.
        Shadows are naughty reflections,

        so is the child to the parent.
Kids are autopsies of their parents.
    By time he's chewing down the third photo

he isn't looking so well.   What's wrong?
    He begins throwing up until he stops moving.
We are all allergic to ourselves, that's why we die.

man like Kenneth.

my man's mum keeps crying like her son was a nice person or
            sutt'n

we all turned up, like we liked him or sutt'n

now he's on a t shirt, grinning over angel wings, they remixed his
            history, now he's an angel all of a sudden

remember when he boxed the birthday girl all of a sudden?

didn't his mum chase us with a cleaver or sutt'n?

too hench and too emotional chattin'

the way he died was typical Kenneth

he saw me at the dance, acted like I was nuff'n

SMALL VICTORIES

I won the award for best acceptance speech.
My stylist is on the run for killing my latest look.
Everything's bless. Rumour is I'm running
for Prime Minister. My long-distance assassin has been
out of office for weeks. They got my birthday wrong
in the news so I'm receiving presents on the wrong day.
I got a birthday cake that tasted like a Monday.
On Tuesday, a delivery man handed me an envelope.
Inside it was a photo of me opening the door to him.
I clawed a wedge of cake into my mouth
and as my tastebuds dilated I had a sense
my assassin had gotten closer. But the cake was so good
I had to close my eyes. I save the rest until
my actual birthday when I hear a knock on the door
and it's my friend Rachel who died when she was 20.
She's ready to swap places.

THE LATE FRIEND

I'm the only person waiting for the tube to Heathrow Terminal 3.
I am late to bury my friend. Thankfully they won't know I'm late.
The train arrives and every seat is taken by the same pilot fifty times.
Turning pages and coughing in sync. One pilot turns to another,

>Why do you think Christ was crucified in the shape
>   of an aeroplane?
>Because his killer was a Pilate.

My friend's funeral is in another timezone. By the time I get there
it will be yesterday. And he'll still be at McDonald's
waiting for me, with a Nike tick of Big Mac sauce on his cheek.
I begin composing an email of apology.
Subject: I'll be with you as soon as I can.

OI YOU LOT

Adefola is hiding a MAC-10 in her weave.
When she dutty whines she accidentally shoots
three people. That was the wickedest whine
of all time, I said to my friends.
My friends have kitchens in their jackets.
I have a living room in my eyes.
Next summer when gunfingers turn into handguns
I'll invite the whole world to my party
and nobody will take their coats off.
When dem boys in coats dance
they sound like food hitting a bin.
And what I thought was the sound of the air
ambulance is really the ceiling fan in heaven.

PORTRAIT OF A MAN
after Wislawa Szymborska

When Ryan asked me what's the current male suicide rate
I said I don't know what man are charging these days.

    Him: Do you always have to make everything a joke?

    Me: I'm a window, I'm transparent even when I'm not open.

I should have said:

        Pangea means our world has already fallen apart.
        A door is just a window that has been to therapy.
        In my hands I present all the space I have
        to hold myself. Would you please
        show me how much space you have?

SHUBZ

Even if everybody at this house party serves a different
god, we all have one devil to share. The plural of
paradise is parody. In God's hands, I'm a wet bar of soap.
I'm in the hallway, bouncing around like a pulse in a
finger. While opening a door I had no business opening,
I see Aunty melting Satan away with a prayer as our
mouths glow with jollof, as we bun piff in the garden.
We find a dildo in Aunty's room later and respect her
more from that day. Esther sees me and says, *Ah, the
church boy has come to the dark side?* Didn't David leave
a trail of clothes as he danced? Didn't a burning bush
bring God to Moses? The heart has chambers and the
brain has pathways, so I am made of water and hallways.
Jesus can either walk all over me or straight through me.

SIDE EFFECTS

You may want to become a piece of art and
hang yourself   start seeing babies
that look like you   spend money
before it goes cold   dream of colonising the sky
You flip a coin and money rolls its eyes
at your chances   think you can sing just because
you're in pain   vision may go blurry
You see halos above the heads of dogs
think your passport photo is your supermodel face
carry your diagnosis like a fur coat in summer
watch a pigeon drink its reflection

AGE

It's a tragedy when your entourage manage
your image, a voyage through your lineage
leads to no village, your wage ain't major,
smoking cabbage, a right of passage. It's a tragedy
when your language has no message. A beige
marriage and a mortgage. It's a tragedy, lager
and jäger the voltage in your beverage.
You were held hostage as a teenager and your outrage
is contagious, and you're a homage to camouflage.

I EXPECT THE WORLD TO END
LIKE THIS

Doors opening for me like the buildings are sneezing.
Skepta on top of a mountain. He says, everyone's happy

about dying, that's why our skulls are smiling. My friends

are planets – when I look up I am dazzled by my darkness.
I expect the world to end like this: I find my young self

and say, Child of divorce, division is what multiplied you.

Only kidding. I spit in his face, leave him forever
playing catch up. I expect the world to end like this:

a zoot just sparked, a couple friends,

we've made dinner tables out of our laps. One friend turns
to me and says, I wish you were here, Kareem.

HELIUM

The way two mirrors make a room bigger,
self reflection tricks you into growing.

The best thing to know about a person
is the worst thing about them.

We are a gang of helium balloons
acting like buoys in the sea.

I rang Selom and said,
we should make punk music.

He said, I'm worried about you,
and it saved my life.

I'm looking for a place to propose

please let me know if you have any
private rooms that lead to private
countries any spare horizons in boxes
or if you have any land to be turned
into a nation for two a room with a
window that moves on the wall as the
sun moves

AFTER ROGER

And if I speak of paradise I speak of ice cold
champagne in my palm, your fat head poking out
from under my arm like a bouquet from a fist.
I speak of my bredrins, unofficial cousins, chosen family
who don't know their faces are holiday destinations.
Your smile is the hammock that could cure insomnia.
Your right eye holding me like a grandparent.
The percussion of your laughter, a secret knock that opens
me.
Like hummingbirds at the edge of a flower, I kiss your
foreheads
and on days when you are far from me I tell the wind to
bring you back,
my nostrils big as biceps.

And if I speak of paradise I speak of my Grandad,
who said to take fun seriously.
A gardener who planted the seed first then prayed for rain.
My grandfather who springloaded his face with the words of God,
spat at demons until their skins fell off.
Who told me God needs friends too,
so if he ever takes one of yours you have to understand,
fill your mouth with good words about them,
rub your belly like a genie's lamp.
The sky belongs to everybody and everybody belongs to the sky.
When the genie comes out, wish for late buses
and missed trains, and beers on benches,
because when someone is gone, they are gone.

And if I speak of paradise I speak of my Grandma,
whose prayers follow me like private investigators.
My Grandma, a nurse who delivered babies
like me. How lucky we all were
to see her first, her face shining into ours like a lamp
onto a desk. My Grandma lives
on God's face, she is his second nose,
used for sniffing out evil.
My Grandma recruited my guardian angel.
She held interviews in Leicester, made sure
they weren't afraid of the dark, knew
how to pump a bike tyre. Must be good
with kids, must resist temptation to be seen.
I pray I never meet my guardian angel, but if I do,
their face will be a collage of my friends.
And if the day comes when I do not have my Grandma
anymore, I will show her picture to newborns
all over the country until they stop crying.

And when I speak of paradise I speak of my phone
autocorrecting buffting to buffeting
and I'm reminded of when man like Ahmed
                    (who we used to call Arm Leg)
said paradise is just bufftings on a plate
as in there is so much to take your pick from
bufftings glazed in oils bufftings on ice warm bufftings spicy
    bufftings

I get to paradise and see Ahmed
swimming in bosoms, buttocks and banter
and he says Kareem wagwan? Where's your tings?
and I say I don't care for all yours
I've got mine right here

SPLIT

after Gboyega Odubanjo, after César Vallejo

I will live in the same town as a bunch of my clones
We will gather in the square like bathing pigeons
My body split into many bodies It is impossible for me to die
I'm surrounded by so much me every reflection in town is a movie
of my faces He has been here for centuries they'll say
invasive species they may call me danger
to the wildlife but I'm just living my life my G
How much more of him is there to come they say
We cannot handle any more it is impossible we are
overflowing the streets are slippery with him

ACKNOWLEDGEMENTS

'SPLIT' has appeared in bath magg issue 13.

Big Ups:

Big up my Family.
My Apple, Rukhsar Ahmed. I love you big time.

Big up: Kieron Rennie, Indigo Williams, Daisy
Dockrill, Lisa Mead, Joelle Taylor, Kayo Chingonyi,
Miriam Nash, Zia Ahmed, Yomi Ṣode, Malika
Booker, Roger Robinson, Jill Abrams, Rishi
Dastidar, Inua Ellams, Aamir Hira, Selom Tevie,
Lorenzo Landicho, Craig Debrah, Jack Prideaux,
Ron Villanueva, Peter Kahn, Tania Nwachukwu,
Tobi Kyeremateng, Michelle Femi Tiwo, Tyrone
Lewis, Tristan Fynn-Aiduenu, Jemilea Wisdom-
Baako, Shadé Joseph, Tice Cin, Belinda Zhawi,
Hibaq Osman, Bayan Goudarzpour, Amina Jama,
Sarah Lasoye, Remi Graves, Nick Makoha, Spread
The Word, Raheela Suleman, FreeWord Centre,
Daisy Henwood, Lewis Buxton, Mandisa Apena,
Darius McFarlane, Jasmine Cooray, Anna Kahn,
Joshua Judson, Lauren Monaghan-Pisano, Rachel
Long, Raymond Antrobus, Jeremiah 'Sugar J'
Brown, Gabriel Akamo, David Vujanic, Victoria
Adukwei Bulley, Peter deGraft-Johnson, Rachel

Long, Be Manzini, Caroline Bird, Aisling Fahey, Jolade Olusanya, Olivia Douglass, Caleb Femi, George Mpanga, Oshanti Ahmed, Zahrah Sheikh, Laurie Ogden, Lionheart, Anita Barton-Williams, Ruth Sutoyé, Ben Willens, Caleb Azumah Nelson, Desree, Tasneim Zyada, Cai Draper, Fahad Al-Amoudi, Courtney Conrad, Antonia Jade King, Amy Acre, Jake Wild Hall. Big up Tate Collective. Big up Barbican Young Poets. Jacob Sam-La Rose, you changed everything for me.

Big up Rachel Ohene-Akrasi. Big up Gboyega Odubanjo.